GAO

United States Government Account

Report to the Ranking
Subcommittee on He
Labor, and Pensions, Co
Education and the Workforce, House of
Representatives

February 2012

DEFINED BENEFIT PENSION PLANS

Recent Developments Highlight Challenges of Hedge Fund and Private Equity Investing

GAO

Accountability ★ Integrity ★ Reliability

GAO-12-324

DEFINED BENEFIT PENSION PLANS

Recent Developments Highlight Challenges of Hedge Fund and Private Equity Investing

Highlights of GAO-12-324, a report to the Ranking Member, Subcommittee on Health, Employment, Labor, and Pensions, Committee on Education and the Workforce, House of Representatives

Why GAO Did This Study

Millions of Americans rely on defined benefit pension plans for their financial well-being in retirement. Plan representatives are increasingly investing in a wide range of assets, including hedge funds and private equity funds. In recent years, GAO has noted that plans may face significant challenges and risks when investing in these alternative assets. These challenges and ongoing market volatility have raised concerns about how these investments have performed since 2008.

As requested, to better understand plan sponsors' experiences with these investments, GAO examined (1) the recent experiences of pension plans with investments in hedge funds and private equity, including lessons learned; (2) how plans have responded to these lessons; and (3) steps federal agencies and other entities have taken to help plan sponsors make and manage these alternative investments.

To answer these questions, GAO analyzed available data; interviewed relevant federal agencies and industry experts; conducted follow-up interviews with 22 public and private pension plan sponsors selected among the top 200 plans and contacted in the course of GAO's prior related work; and surveyed 20 plan consultants, academic experts and other industry experts.

This report reemphasizes a 2008 recommendation that the Secretary of Labor provide guidance to help plans investing in hedge funds and private equity.

View GAO-12-324. For more information, contact Charles Jeszeck at (202) 512-7215 or jeszeckc@gao.gov.

What GAO Found

While plan representatives GAO contacted generally stated that their hedge fund and private equity investments met expectations in recent years, a number of plans experienced losses and other challenges, such as limited liquidity and transparency. National data indicated that hedge fund and private equity investments were significantly affected by the 2008-2009 financial crisis, and plans and experts GAO contacted indicated that pension plan investments were not insulated from losses. Most of the 22 plan representatives GAO interviewed said that their hedge fund investments met expectations overall, despite, in some cases, significant losses during the financial crisis. A few plan representatives, however, expected hedge fund investments to be much more resilient in turbulent markets, and found the losses disappointing. Given the long-term nature of private equity investments, almost all of the representatives were generally satisfied with these investments over the last 5 years. Some plan representatives described significant difficulties in hedge fund and private equity investing related to limited liquidity and transparency, and the negative impact of the actions of other investors in the fund—sometimes referred to as co-investors. For example, representatives from one plan reported they were unable to cash out of their hedge fund investments due to discretionary withdrawal restrictions imposed by the fund manager, requiring them to sell some of their stock holdings at a severe loss in order to pay plan benefits.

Most plans included in our review have taken actions to address challenges related to their hedge fund and private equity investments, including allocation reductions, modifications of investment terms, and improvements to the fund selection and monitoring process. National data reveal that plans have continued to invest in hedge funds and private equity—for example, one survey revealed that the percentage of large plans investing in hedge funds grew from 47 percent in 2007 to 60 percent in 2010—and most plans GAO contacted have also maintained or increased their allocations to these investments. However, most plans have adjusted investment strategies as a result of recent years' experiences. For example, three plans have reduced their allocations to hedge funds or private equity. Other plan representatives also took steps to improve investment terms, including more favorable fee structures and enhanced liquidity. However, some plan representatives and experts indicated that smaller plans would likely not be able to take some of these steps.

The Department of Labor has provided some guidance to plans regarding investing in derivatives, but has not taken any steps specifically related to hedge fund and private equity investments. In recent years, however, other entities have addressed this issue. For example, in 2009, the President's Working Group on Financial Markets issued best practices for hedge fund investors. Further, both GAO and a Department of Labor advisory body have recommended that the department publish guidance for plans that invest in such alternative assets. To date, it has not done so, in part because of a concern that the lack of uniformity among such investments could make development of useful guidance difficult. In 2011, the Department of Labor advisory body specifically revisited the issue of pension plans' investments in hedge funds and private equity, and a report is expected in early 2012.

Contents

Abbreviations

Dodd-Frank Act	Dodd-Frank Wall Street Reform and Consumer Protection Act
ERISA	Employee Retirement Income Security Act
ILPA	Institutional Limited Partners Association
IOPS	International Organisation of Pension Supervisors
Labor	Department of Labor
OECD	Organisation for Economic Cooperation and Development
SEC	Securities and Exchange Commission

United States Government Accountability Office
Washington, DC 20548

February 16, 2012

The Honorable Robert E. Andrews
Ranking Member
Subcommittee on Health, Employment, Labor,
    and Pensions
Committee on Education and the Workforce
House of Representatives

Dear Mr. Andrews:

Millions of Americans rely on defined benefit pension plans for their financial well-being in retirement. In order to pay promised retirement benefits when due and at an acceptable cost, employers must make adequate contributions to these funds, and plan fiduciaries must invest the fund balance in assets that yield an adequate rate of return over time. Public and private sector pension plans have primarily invested in traditional investments such as stocks and bonds, but plans are increasingly investing in "alternative" investments such as hedge funds and private equity funds.

Generally, hedge funds and private equity funds are privately organized and managed funds that are available only to institutional investors or wealthy individuals. Historically, both have been managed in ways that exempt them from certain aspects of federal securities law and regulation that apply to other investment pools such as mutual funds. However, as a result of the Dodd-Frank Wall Street Reform and Consumer Protection Act (Dodd-Frank Act),[1] most hedge fund and private equity managers will be required to register with the Securities and Exchange Commission (SEC) and comply with new aspects of federal securities law.

Much has happened in the financial markets since GAO issued a report in 2008 examining the extent to which pension plans invest in hedge funds

---

[1]Pub. L. No. 111-203, 124 Stat. 1376 (2010).

and private equity.[2] The financial market events of the second half of 2008 significantly affected hedge funds. According to a 2009 industry survey, most hedge fund strategies produced double-digit losses in 2008, and hedge funds saw approximately $70 billion in redemptions between June and November 2008.[3] Nevertheless, many of these investments have rebounded, and a 2010 industry survey of institutional investors suggests that these investors continue to be committed to investing in hedge funds but with a shifting set of objectives and criteria.[4] Private equity investment values were also substantially lowered during this period and have similarly recovered along with values in the public equities market. However, given ongoing market volatility, concerns remain about how well such investments will meet the expectations of plan sponsors that have invested in them.

In order to assess the extent to which pension plans have realized desired benefits from investing in hedge funds and private equity, and actions they may have taken in response to recent experiences, particularly given ongoing market volatility, you asked us to examine the following questions:

- What is known about the experiences of defined benefit pension plans with investments in hedge funds and private equity, including recent lessons learned?

- How have plan sponsors responded to lessons learned from recent experiences with such alternative investments?

---

[2]This report, GAO, *Defined Benefit Pension Plans: Guidance Needed to Better Inform Plans of the Challenges and Risks of Investing in Hedge Funds and Private Equity*, GAO-08-692, (Washington, D.C.: Aug.14, 2008), was followed by other GAO documents reflecting more recent data in 2010 and 2011. These documents were *Defined Benefit Pension Plans: Plans Face Valuation and Other Challenges When Investing in Hedge Funds and Private Equity*, GAO-10-915T (Washington, D.C.: July 20, 2010) and *Defined Benefit Pension Plans, Plans Face Challenges When Investing in Hedge Funds and Private Equity*, GAO-11-901SP (Washington, D.C.: Aug. 31, 2011).

[3]Greenwich Associates and SEI Knowledge Partnership, *Hedge Funds under the Microscope: Examining Institutional Commitment in Challenging Times* (January 2009).

[4]Greenwich Associates and SEI Knowledge Partnership, *Institutional Hedge Fund Investing Comes of Age: A New Perspective on the Road Ahead* (June 2011).

GAO-12-324 Defined Benefit Pension Plans

- What steps have federal agencies and other entities taken to help plan sponsors make and manage investments in such alternative assets, and what additional steps might be warranted?

To answer these questions, we reviewed relevant literature; analyzed data; interviewed relevant federal agencies and industry experts; conducted in-depth, follow-up interviews with pension plan sponsors contacted in the course of our prior related work; and surveyed a selected group of 20 plan consultants, academic experts, and other industry experts. Specifically, we conducted in-depth, follow-up interviews with representatives of 22 public and private sector defined benefit pension plans that were interviewed for our 2008 report examining the extent to which pension plans invest in hedge funds and private equity.[5] We identified these plans in 2008 using data from the 2006 *Pensions & Investments* survey of the largest 200 pension plans and through our interviews with industry experts. Plan representatives' responses from these interviews do not represent a statistically generalizeable sample of all pension plans. We interviewed officials of federal agencies, relevant national organizations, pension plan consulting firms, and other national experts. We conducted a survey of five open-ended questions with plan consultants, academic and industry experts, representatives of plan participants, and representatives of public and private plan sponsors. We obtained data on the national performance of hedge fund and private equity investments from private organizations, Cambridge Associates LLC and Hedge Fund Research, Inc. We obtained and analyzed survey data on the extent to which pension plan sponsors continue to invest in hedge funds and private equity from two private organizations, Greenwich Associates and *Pensions & Investments*. We conducted our work from February 2011 to February 2012 in accordance with generally accepted government auditing standards. Those standards require that we plan and perform the audit to obtain sufficient, appropriate evidence to provide a reasonable basis for our findings and conclusions based on our audit objectives. We believe that the evidence obtained provides a reasonable basis for our findings and conclusions based on our audit objectives. For more information on our objectives, scope, and methodology, see appendix I.

---

[5]GAO-08-692.

Background

Defined benefit pension plans are intended to pay retirement benefits that are generally based on an employee's years of service and other factors. The financial condition of these plans—and hence their ability to pay retirement benefits when due—depends on adequate contributions from employers and sometimes employees, and prudent investments that yield an adequate rate of return over time. Poor investment choices can have serious implications for both the plan sponsor and, potentially, plan beneficiaries. Poor investment results may necessitate greater contributions by the plan sponsor, which could result in lower profits in the case of a private plan sponsor, or higher taxes in the case of a public plan. In some cases, the plan sponsor could opt to require greater participant contributions or reduce future retiree benefits. Plan sponsors generally try to maximize returns for an acceptable level of risk and, in doing so, may invest in various categories of asset classes, which for many years have consisted mainly of stocks and bonds. Plan sponsors may also invest in other asset classes or trading strategies, sometimes referred to as alternative investments—which can include a wide range of assets such as hedge funds, private equity, real estate, and commodities. Plans may make such investments in an effort to diversify their portfolios, achieve higher returns or for other reasons. In recent years, hedge funds and private equity have been two of the most common alternative assets held by institutional investors such as public and private pension plans.

Although there is no universally accepted definition of hedge funds, the term is commonly used to describe pooled investment vehicles that are privately organized and administered by professional managers who often engage in active trading of various types of securities, commodity futures, options contracts, and other investment vehicles.[6] Hedge funds can also hold relatively illiquid and hard-to-value investments such as real estate or shares in private equity funds. Although hedge funds have a reputation of being risky investments that seek exceptional returns, this was not their original purpose, and is not true of all hedge funds today. Established in the 1940s, one of the first hedge funds invested in equities and used leverage and short selling to protect, or "hedge" the portfolio from its

---

[6]In both the hedge fund and private equity industries, the entity that is responsible for management of the fund is commonly referred to as the general partner, and an investor in the fund is commonly referred to as a limited partner. In this report, except where other terminology is appropriate, we refer the general partner as the fund manager, and the limited partners as co-investors.

exposure to the stock market.[7] Over time, hedge funds diversified their investment portfolios and engaged in a wider variety of investments strategies. As GAO reported in 2008, defined benefit pension plans have invested in hedge funds for a number of reasons, including the desire for investment returns that exceed the returns available in the stock market or obtaining steadier, less volatile returns.

Likewise, there is no commonly accepted definition of private equity funds, but such funds are generally privately managed pools of capital that invest in companies, many of which are not listed on a stock exchange. Unlike many hedge funds, private equity funds typically make longer-term investments in private companies. Private equity funds also seek to obtain financial returns through long-term appreciation based on active management. Strategies of private equity funds vary, but most funds target either venture capital or buy-out opportunities. Venture capital funds invest in young companies that often are developing a new product or technology. Private equity fund managers may provide expertise to a fledgling company to help it become suitable for an initial public offering. Buy-out funds generally invest in larger established companies in order to add value, in part, by increasing efficiencies and, in some cases, consolidating resources by merging complementary businesses or technologies. For both venture capital and buy-out strategies, investors hope to profit when the company is eventually sold, either when offered to the public or when sold to another investor or company. Unlike stocks and bonds, which are traded and priced in public markets, plans have limited information on the value of private equity investments until the underlying holdings are sold.

Traditionally, hedge funds and private equity funds and their managers have been exempt from certain registration, disclosure and other requirements under various federal securities laws. The presumption is that investors in such vehicles have the sophistication to understand the risks involved in investing in them and the resources to absorb any losses they may suffer. However, as a result of the Dodd-Frank Act, the managers of such investment vehicles will be regulated in ways that they

---

[7]Leverage involves the use of borrowed money or other techniques to potentially increase an investments' value or return without increasing the capital invested. A short sale is the sale of a security that the seller does not own or a sale that is consummated by the delivery of a security borrowed by, or for, the account of the seller. Short selling is generally used to profit by the decline in the price of a security.

have not been previously.[8] For example, hedge fund and private equity managers will generally now be required to register with the SEC, establish a specific regulatory compliance program, and comply with various record-keeping requirements.[9] While these fund managers must now register with the SEC, the funds they manage will remain unregistered. Unlike other investment funds—such as mutual funds—that register with the SEC, hedge funds and private equity funds are thus not subject to certain requirements, such as limitations on leverage and minimum requirements relating to corporate governance.

Private sector pension plan investment decisions must comply with provisions of Employee Retirement Income Security Act (ERISA), which set forth fiduciary standards based on the principle of a prudent standard of care. Under ERISA, plan sponsors and other fiduciaries must (1) act solely in the interest of the plan participants and beneficiaries and in accordance with plan documents; (2) invest with the care, skill, and diligence of a prudent person familiar with such matters; and (3) diversify plan investments to minimize the risk of large losses. Under ERISA, the prudence of any individual investment is considered in the context of the total plan portfolio, rather than in isolation.[10] Public sector plans, such as those at the state, county, and municipal levels, are not subject to funding, vesting, and most other requirements applicable to private sector defined benefit pension plans under ERISA, but must follow requirements established for them under applicable state law. Many states have enacted standards comparable to those of ERISA.

---

[8]15 U.S.C. § 80b-20 note, section 401-419 of the Dodd-Frank Wall Street Reform and Consumer Protection Act (Pub. L. No. 111-203, 124 Stat. 1376 (2010)).

[9]Some hedge fund and private equity managers will remain exempt under the new law. For example, certain fund managers with less than $150 million in assets under management will not be required to register with the SEC. Exemption for Advisers to Venture Capital Funds with Less than $150 Million in Assets Under Management, and Foreign Private Advisers No. 57-37-10, 76 Fed. Reg. 39646 (2011).

[10]ERISA's "prudent man" standard with respect to investment duties is treated under 29 C.F.R. § 2550.404a-1(b). In general, it provides that that the prudent man standard is satisfied if the fiduciary has given appropriate consideration, among other facts and circumstances, to the following factors (1) the composition of the plan portfolio with regard to diversification of risk; (2) the volatility of the plan investment portfolio with regard to general movements of investment prices; (3) the liquidity of the plan investment portfolio relative to the funding objectives of the plan; (4) the projected return of the plan investment portfolio relative to the funding objectives of the plan; and (5) the prevailing and projected economic conditions of the entities in which the plan has invested and proposes to invest.

In 2008, we reported on plan investments in hedge funds and private equity, including a discussion of the benefits that plan fiduciaries seek and challenges they face in doing so. We concluded that, because these investments require a degree of fiduciary effort well beyond that required by more traditional investments, doing so can be a difficult challenge, especially for smaller plans. Such plans may not have the expertise or financial resources to be fully aware of these challenges, or have the ability to address them through negotiation, due diligence, and monitoring. Further, we noted that, while plans are responsible for making prudent choices when investing in any asset, the Department of Labor (Labor) also has a role in helping to ensure that pension plan sponsors fulfill their fiduciary duties in managing pension plans that are subject to ERISA. This can include educating employers and service providers about their fiduciary responsibilities under ERISA. In light of these duties, and the risks and challenges of investing in hedge funds and private equity, we recommended that the Secretary of Labor issue guidance specifically designed for qualified plans under ERISA. We specifically called for guidance that would (1) outline the unique challenges of investing in hedge funds and private equity; (2) describe steps that plans should take to address these challenges and help meet ERISA requirements; and (3) explain the implications of these challenges and steps for smaller plans. To date, Labor has not implemented this recommendation. In responding to GAO's 2008 recommendation, Labor noted that while it would consider the recommendation, the lack of uniformity among hedge funds and private equity funds could make development of comprehensive and useful guidance difficult.

Selected Pension Plans Reported Mixed Experiences with Hedge Funds and Private Equity Investments, and Some Faced Significant Losses and Other Challenges

Hedge Fund and Private Equity Investments Were Affected by the Financial Crisis, but Most Selected Plans Indicated These Investments Met Expectations

Hedge fund and private equity indexes show that these investments were significantly affected by the financial market turbulence of recent years, and plans and experts we contacted indicated that pension plan investments were not insulated from losses. According to a composite hedge fund index, in the midst of the financial crisis, hedge funds produced quarterly losses as great as 16 percent in the last quarter of 2008.[11] Similarly, a private equity index measured losses throughout most of 2008, with losses of a little more than 15 percent in the last quarter.[12] In comparison, the stock market, as measured by the Standard and Poor's 500 index, declined in value by close to 40 percent in 2008 (see table 1 for a comparison of recent data from various indexes). Our in-depth discussions with plan representatives were largely consistent with these national trends. Although not all plan sponsor representatives we interviewed reported specific performance data, a number of plan representatives disclosed peak annual hedge fund losses in 2008 or 2009 ranging from about 12 percent to about 25 percent. Pension plan representatives we interviewed generally reported more favorable performance for private equity. Although a few plan representatives reported private equity returns that were somewhat lower than in previous

---

[11]Hedge Fund Research, Inc., HFRI Fund Weighted Composite Index. According to this index, hedge funds produced quarterly losses in 3 of the 4 quarters in 2008.

[12]Cambridge Associates LLC, U.S. Private Equity Index, June 30, 2011. The index is an end-to-end calculation based on data compiled from 899 U.S. private equity funds (buyout, growth equity, private equity energy, and mezzanine funds), including fully liquidated partnerships, formed between 1986 and 2011.

years, one plan reported a close to 20 percent loss for their private equity portfolio in 2009.

Table 1: Recent Data from Hedge Fund, Private Equity, and S&P 500 Indexes

Index	Historical performance (in percentages)		
	1 year (2011)	3 year (2009-2011)	5 year (2007-2011)
HFRI Fund Weighted Composite	(5.02)	7.9	2.27
Cambridge Private Equity	13.76	7.32	8.11
S&P 500	2.11	14.11	(0.25)

Sources: Hedge Fund Research, Inc., HFRI Fund Weighted Composite Index; Cambridge Associates LLC, U.S. Private Equity Index; and S&P 500 Index.

Note: Numbers in parentheses are negative. Hedge Fund Research, Inc., HFRI Fund Weighted Composite Index and S&P 500 Index data are as of December 31, 2011. Cambridge Associates LLC, U.S. Private Equity Index data are as of September 30, 2011.

Despite experiencing some significant losses during the financial crisis, representatives of selected plan sponsors we contacted generally told us that both their hedge fund and private equity investments met their expectations over the last 5 years given their reasons for investing.

Hedge Funds

Most of the 22 pension plan representatives we contacted indicated that hedge fund investments met their expectations given their reasons for investing. In 2008, we reported that many plans had invested in hedge funds in response to prior significant stock market losses, and because they were seeking specific benefits such as achieving (1) lower volatility; (2) a more diversified portfolio by investing in a vehicle that would not be correlated with other asset classes in the portfolio; and (3) returns greater than those expected in the stock market. Given these reasons for investing in hedge funds, most of the 22 plan representatives we interviewed for this report said that these investments met plan expectations (see table 2 for an overview of the responses).

Table 2: Performance of Hedge Fund and Private Equity Investments Compared to Selected Plans' Expectations

	Number of plans	
Plan response	Hedge fund	Private equity
Met expectations	12	20
Did not meet expectations	5	0
Mixed	1	2
Total	**18**	**22**

Source: GAO analysis of interview responses.

Note: Four plans we interviewed had not invested in hedge funds when we interviewed them for our 2008 report and therefore could not provide an assessment.

Representatives of several plans stressed the moderating impact of hedge fund investments by noting their ability to provide less price volatility than other investments. One plan representative observed, that even with hedge fund fees, their losses of 14 percent were still preferable to stock market losses of 40 percent. Representatives from another plan explained that, although hedge fund performance more closely paralleled the stock market during the period than desired, there was generally no safe haven and that hedge fund investments have generally performed well. A few plan representatives noted that hedge funds delivered lower volatility than other investments.[13] Representatives from one plan were particularly satisfied with how the plan's hedge fund investments helped limit overall portfolio risks, noting that although returns were below benchmarks, the hedge funds provided much less volatility than the plan's publicly traded stock holdings. Similarly, representatives from another plan noted that, since 2002, hedge funds have provided adequate returns, but with much less volatility than publicly traded stocks. Additionally, representatives from one plan, who had not invested in hedge funds when we interviewed them for our 2008 report, have recently begun implementing a relatively small hedge fund allocation that they

---

[13]Volatility refers to the propensity of the price of a security to move up or down over time; if the price of a security moves up or down rapidly over a short period of time, it is considered to have higher volatility. Stocks offer relatively high expected long-term returns at the risk of considerable volatility, that is, the likelihood of significant short-term losses or gains. Plan sponsor representatives may invest in hedge funds that employ a specific investment strategy to meet plan goals, such as lower volatility. Because some hedge fund strategies are not solely dependent on equity and fixed income markets for their returns, they may produce significantly less volatility.

believe will complement the rest of their portfolio and provide greater diversification benefits, including reducing overall portfolio volatility.

Some plan sponsor representatives stressed the positive long-term performance of their hedge fund investments, despite intervals of poor performance. While these plan representatives would have preferred better hedge fund performance during the 2008-2009 financial crisis, hedge funds have nonetheless filled an important long-term role in these plans' portfolios. Representatives from one plan noted hedge fund losses of about 12 percent during 2009 but indicated that overall since 2004 these investments have performed well. Representatives from one plan told us that while they were disappointed by the size of hedge fund losses in 2008-2009, these investments have generally beaten long-term benchmarks and have recovered since the crisis. Moreover, they noted that compounded over the last 15 years, the plan's hedge fund investment returns are about twice those of the stock market. These plan representatives also emphasized the importance of hedge funds, as well as other alternative investments, to long-term investment returns by noting that investing solely in fixed income investments would not have sustained the plan's funding needs, particularly given that the plan sponsor had not made plan contributions in over 20 years.

In contrast, a number of plan sponsor representatives and experts noted that hedge funds did not perform as expected. Representatives from one plan explained that they expected these investments to provide an absolute return—positive return regardless of the conditions in the stock market—in exchange for muted returns in robust markets. Another plan representative noted that while he understood these "absolute return" funds may not always generate positive returns in all market environments, he expected their hedge funds to deliver better than the more than 20 percent losses they experienced from 2008-2009. Similarly, a representative from one plan expected hedge fund investments to perform more independently of stock market trends and was surprised and disappointed by the magnitude of the negative returns. This representative told us that for every dollar of loss in the 2008-2009 stock market, their hedge fund investments lost two-thirds of a dollar. A few experts noted that pension plan hedge fund investments were more correlated than expected with the public markets during the financial crisis, resulting in what one expert referred to as exacerbated losses. For example, one expert noted that some plan representatives may have overpaid for mediocre returns when they paid hedge fund performance and management fees to obtain returns similar to the stock market.[14] Further, one specific hedge fund strategy performed poorly. Several plans singled out the so-called "portable alpha" strategy, which typically employs hedge funds in order to generate returns that exceed common market benchmarks.[15] A representative of one plan told us that the plan's portable alpha program was hugely disappointing and consequently being dismantled. Specifically, in 2008-2009, a portion of the investment lost considerable value when the stock market fell by more than 30 percent.

Some plan representatives and one surveyed expert singled out the impact of fees on net performance. One expert cited the extra layer of fees charged by funds of funds managers, asserting that these fees substantially lowered plans' net returns.[16] Similarly, a plan representative we spoke with found hedge fund fees at the individual fund level to be eroding investment returns. This representative noted while the plan's hedge fund gross return has been outperforming the rest of the portfolio, the investment has underperformed after fees have been deducted for the last few years. For this reason, the plan is consciously lowering its investment allocation in hedge funds. A representative from another plan noted dissatisfaction with the plan's hedge fund of funds investment as one of the reasons that the plan had chosen not to reinvest and was considering firing the fund manager.

Private Equity

The experience of plans with private equity investments should be considered in the context of the long-term nature of these investments, which require lengthy financial commitments and delayed financial returns (see fig. 1). Given the long-term nature of private equity investments,

---

[14]Whereas mutual fund managers reportedly charge a fee of about 1 percent of assets under management, hedge fund managers often charge a flat fee of 2 percent of total assets under management, plus a performance fee, of about 20 percent of the fund's profits. While this fee structure may vary slightly among funds, it has been a common structure in both the hedge fund and private equity industries.

[15]The portable alpha strategy is designed to deliver better returns than traditional benchmarks. Typically, the strategy involves using derivatives to replicate benchmark returns (beta), which leaves excess cash that can be invested in hedge fund strategies to obtain returns above the stock market (alpha).

[16]Funds of funds' managers charge fees above those of the hedge fund manager. For example, funds of funds managers may charge a 1 percent flat fee and a performance fee of between 5 and 10 percent of profits—on top of the substantial fees that the fund of funds pays to the underlying hedge funds.

nearly all of the 22 pension plan representatives we interviewed were generally satisfied with their private equity investments over the last 5 years. Based on findings from our 2008 report, plans we interviewed generally invested in private equity to attain higher returns than the stock market offered, in exchange for greater risk. Given these reasons for investing in private equity, 20 of 22 plan representatives reported that the plan's private equity investments met plan expectations. Further, nearly half of plan representatives indicated that their plans' private equity investments outperformed public equities over the last 5 years. For at least one plan, private equity was the highest performing asset class. In particular, several plan representatives and surveyed experts noted that opportunistic investments, those investments that take advantage of underperformance during market cycles, such as distressed debt, performed relatively well during the last 5 years.[17] Representatives from at least one plan said they were disappointed to have had insufficient capital available to invest more heavily in some of these opportunities. Like many of the plan representatives we interviewed, experts we surveyed largely found private equity investment performance for the period to be positive.

---

[17]A few plan officials indicated that opportunistic private equity investments such as distressed debt are shorter in duration than traditional private equity investments, such as leveraged buy-outs and venture capital. For example, private equity distressed debt investment involves the fund purchasing severely discounted corporate bonds of companies that have filed for bankruptcy or appear likely to do so in order to become a major creditor. The fund is then positioned to control the company's liquidation or reorganization. In the event of a bankruptcy, as a major creditor, the fund will likely recover all their money, if not a profit, as part of the liquidation of assets. Alternatively, in a typically more desirable outcome, the company will reorganize and come out of bankruptcy, and the fund will forgive the company's debt obligation in exchange for enough equity to compensate them.

Figure 1: Typical Private Equity Long-term Investment Profile

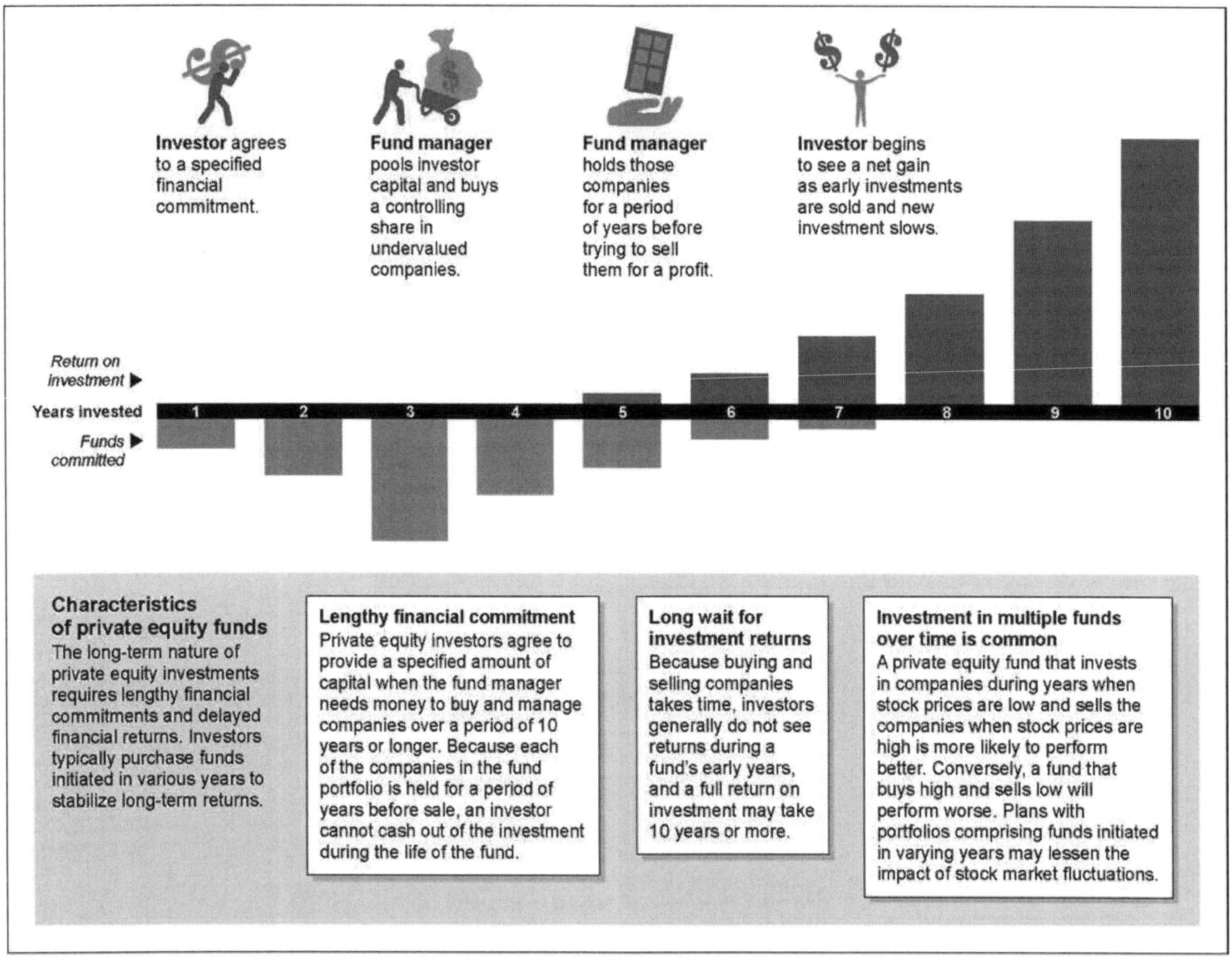

Investor agrees to a specified financial commitment.

Fund manager pools investor capital and buys a controlling share in undervalued companies.

Fund manager holds those companies for a period of years before trying to sell them for a profit.

Investor begins to see a net gain as early investments are sold and new investment slows.

Return on investment ►

Years invested: 1 2 3 4 5 6 7 8 9 10

Funds ► committed

Characteristics of private equity funds
The long-term nature of private equity investments requires lengthy financial commitments and delayed financial returns. Investors typically purchase funds initiated in various years to stabilize long-term returns.

Lengthy financial commitment
Private equity investors agree to provide a specified amount of capital when the fund manager needs money to buy and manage companies over a period of 10 years or longer. Because each of the companies in the fund portfolio is held for a period of years before sale, an investor cannot cash out of the investment during the life of the fund.

Long wait for investment returns
Because buying and selling companies takes time, investors generally do not see returns during a fund's early years, and a full return on investment may take 10 years or more.

Investment in multiple funds over time is common
A private equity fund that invests in companies during years when stock prices are low and sells the companies when stock prices are high is more likely to perform better. Conversely, a fund that buys high and sells low will perform worse. Plans with portfolios comprising funds initiated in varying years may lessen the impact of stock market fluctuations.

Source: GAO analysis of various descriptions of private equity funds.

Note: This information is most relevant to more long-term private equity investments, such as leveraged buy-outs. Other types of private equity investment, such as distressed debt, may have a shorter financial commitment.

Although plan representatives we interviewed almost unanimously reported favorable results regarding private equity, this has not necessarily been true of all plans over the last 5 years. As we reported in 2008, compared with other asset classes, performance varied widely among private equity funds. For this reason, plan representatives emphasized the importance of investing in the top funds, some noting that they would not invest in private equity unless they could invest in funds considered to be in the top quartile. Three of the experts we surveyed in 2011 also noted varying performance among private equity funds. One expert noted a wide dispersion among the performance of private equity funds, and that this dispersion likely is reflective of the broad experiences of pension plans over time. Similarly, two other experts cited evidence that, over the long-term, broad private equity fund returns did not outperform the stock market, and one of these experts reported that lower performance may be attributable to the typically riskier equities held in these investments. A representative from one plan, for example, remarked that the plan's venture capital investments did not perform well. In this particular case involving the biotech industry, the representative noted that this was less a direct result of the financial crisis and more a function of the decline in this industry as a whole. Representatives from one large plan told us that venture capital investment performance had been problematic for them in the last 10 years. Similarly, we found that a number of plans we interviewed had lowered or eliminated their venture capital investment in recent years.

Some Selected Plans Faced Specific Challenges with Hedge Fund and Private Equity Investments in Recent Years

Pension plan representatives we contacted experienced some challenges in hedge fund and private equity investing beyond those of more traditional investing, including limited liquidity and transparency, and the negative impact of the actions of other investors in the fund—sometimes referred to as co-investors.

Liquidity Limitations

A number of plan representatives we interviewed experienced challenges with investment liquidity—a plan's limited ability to redeem investment shares on demand—in order to meet plan obligations. Although hedge funds typically have limitations on the timing and magnitude of investor redemptions, a few plan representatives we contacted were surprised and financially harmed by "discretionary gates"—limitations on redemptions imposed at a fund manager's discretion.[18] For example, a representative from one large plan told us that some hedge fund managers imposed discretionary gates based on what was best for the fund's business model and not what was in the best interests of the investors. This representative was concerned that hedge fund managers lacked incentives to seek returns and were focused on gathering assets, locking them up, and collecting the fees. Public documents from this plan noted the possibility that a hedge fund manager can earn tens of millions of dollars in performance fees in 1 year and then experience sizable losses in another, resulting in only a minimal capital gain or even net loss for the investor, but sizable profits for the fund manager at the end of the partnership.[19] Also, because plan representatives from at least one plan intended to use hedge fund redemptions to pay for plan obligations, unexpected discretionary gates forced them to instead sell public equities at a significant loss. Specifically, representatives from one plan told us that when the market was down more than 30 percent, they were unable to access their hedge fund investments due to gates imposed by the fund manager after other co-investors began liquidating their holdings. Representatives from this plan told us they were then compelled to sell public equities at a price well below their assessment of the equities' intrinsic value, in order to meet plan obligations, including benefit payments to plan participants.

Some plans also faced challenges meeting requests for committed capital—money they have committed to the fund manager for

---

[18]As we reported in 2008, hedge funds offer investors relatively limited liquidity, that is, investors may not be able to redeem a hedge fund investment on demand because of a hedge fund's redemption policy. Hedge funds often require an initial "lockup" of a year or more, during which an investor cannot cash out of the hedge fund. After the initial lockup period, hedge funds offer occasional liquidity, sometimes with a prenotification requirement. Occasional liquidity may be limited by a fund manager's right to limit the amount of redemptions in a stated period. Limitations on redemptions, including discretionary gates, can be important to hedge funds because sudden liquidations could disrupt a carefully calibrated investment strategy and because some of the hedge fund's underlying assets may themselves be illiquid.

[19]The effect of such performance fee structures can be moderated by "clawback" provisions—which provide investors the right to reclaim a portion of a fund manager's performance fee based on significant losses from later investments in the fund's portfolio—in the investment contract. Similarly, "high water mark" provisions can moderate the effect of such performance fee structures by ensuring that investors will not pay a performance fee unless the value of the investment passes a previous peak value of the fund shares.

investment—from private equity fund managers. A few plan representatives relied on a "self funding" private equity program in which private equity investment proceeds are sufficient to pay for a portion or all of the program's committed capital. However, in some cases, the severe market decline during this period limited investment proceeds. Consequently, a few plans had to look for liquidity in their portfolio in order to fund capital commitments. While the plan representatives we spoke with were able to meet these financial commitments, a number of plans said they limited new private equity investment during this period.

Limited Transparency

A small number of plans we interviewed noted challenges with hedge fund transparency during this period. One plan representative we interviewed invested in a fund of hedge funds[20] with very limited transparency, but that promised access to certain high-quality hedge funds. As transparency improved after the 2008-2009 financial crisis, the plan sponsor learned that the various funds of funds had considerable overlapping investments, which likely amplified the funds' of funds negative performance. A few plan representatives were unpleasantly surprised by the extent to which their plans' hedge funds were invested in "side pockets"—separate side accounts holding illiquid investments, such as private equity or real estate. For example, representatives from one plan told us they were not fully aware of the way some of their funds were invested in these side pockets and consequently were surprised by the illiquidity of the investment. A representative from another plan was similarly surprised by how embedded some of their hedge fund investments were with side pockets, which proved problematic when the plan looked to these hedge fund investments for liquidity during the financial crisis and it was not available. Representatives of another plan expressed an aversion to such side pocket investments and preferred to invest in private equity directly rather than doing so unbeknownst to them through a hedge fund manager.

Negative Impact of the Actions of Co-Investors

A few of the plan representatives noted challenges related to co-investors' actions. Under commingled investments arrangements, each

---

[20]Individuals and institutions may also invest in hedge funds through funds of hedge funds, which are investment funds that buy shares of multiple underlying hedge funds. Fund of funds managers invest in other hedge funds rather than trade directly in the financial markets and thus offer investors broader exposure to different hedge fund managers and strategies. Like hedge funds, funds of funds may be exempt from various aspects of federal securities laws and regulations.

investor owns a certain number of shares in a fund. During the recent financial crisis, the significance of these arrangements became particularly challenging for a few plan representatives. For example, representatives from one plan reported that while they were able to meet all of their private equity capital calls—a request from the fund manager for the investors to provide a portion of the money they have committed to investing—they were concerned about the ability of other co-investors to do so. In response to these concerns, the representatives felt compelled to take the time to call each of their fund managers to confirm the ability of all the investors to meet their financial commitments. Representatives of another plan noted that the actions of co-investors can impact an investment strategy, which may ultimately impact returns. For example, representatives of this plan said they had invested with a private equity fund manager who was implementing a strategy involving an investment in 10, $1 billion companies. However, because not all investors could meet their financial commitments, the fund manager had to restructure the investment strategy. The plan representatives were troubled by the strategy changes—involving investments in different companies—the fund manager had to make as a result.

At least one plan representative also indicated that an onslaught of hedge fund redemptions by other co-investors damaged their investments. For example, representatives of one plan told us that many of their co-investors, alarmed by large losses during the financial crisis, moved quickly to cash out investments. Because co-investor redemptions led to further fund losses, plan representatives felt it was necessary to cash out as well. However, they were unable to do so, because the fund manager had imposed a discretionary gate to prevent further losses.

Plans Continue to Invest in Hedge Funds and Private Equity, but Some Plan Sponsors Have Taken Steps to Address Challenges

Available data reveal that plan investments in hedge funds and private equity have continued to increase, and our contacts with 22 public and private defined benefit (DB) plan sponsors also reveal a continued commitment to these investment vehicles. Nonetheless, some plans have reduced their allocations or made significant changes to their strategic approach as a result of experiences in recent years. In addition, plan representatives we contacted took significant steps to improve the terms of their investments, including negotiating lower fees or more advantageous fee terms, and obtaining greater liquidity or transparency. Not all plans may be able to make such improvements, however.

Plans Have Continued to Invest in Hedge Funds and Private Equity

Available data and discussions with plan representatives indicate that DB plans have continued to invest in hedge funds and private equity in recent years. The percentage of large plans investing in both hedge fund and private equity has increased since the onset of the 2008 financial crisis. According to a *Pensions & Investments* survey, the percentage of large plans (as measured by total plan assets) investing in hedge funds grew from 47 percent in 2007 to 60 percent in 2010 (see fig. 2). Over the same time period, the percentage of large plans that invested in private equity also grew—from 80 percent to 92 percent. For both hedge funds and private equity, as figure 2 shows, these trends are a continuation of a decade-long upward trend. Data from the same survey reveal that investments in hedge funds and private equity typically constitute a small share of plan assets. The average allocation of portfolio assets to hedge funds among plans with such investments was a little over 5 percent in 2010. Similarly, among plans with investments in private equity, the average allocation of portfolio assets was a little over 9 percent.

Figure 2: Share of Large DB Plans Investing in Hedge Funds and Private Equity from 2001 to 2010

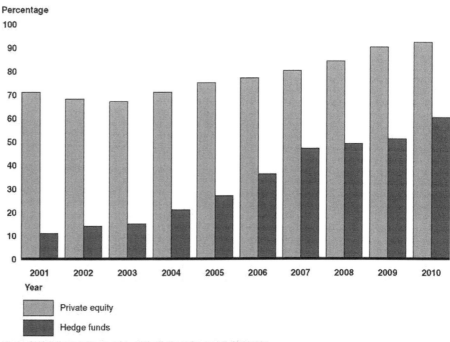

Source: GAO analysis of *Pensions & Investments* annual survey data, 2001-2010.

Note: These data represent plans with $1 billion or more in total assets.

GAO-12-324 Defined Benefit Pension Plans

We reported in 2008 that available survey data showed larger plans were more likely to invest in hedge funds and private equity than midsize plans and, according to a survey by Greenwich Associates, that seemed to be the case in 2010 as well. The survey found that 22 percent of midsize plans—those with $250 million to $500 million in total assets—were invested in hedge funds compared with 40 percent of the largest plans—those with over $5 billion in total assets (see fig. 3). Survey data on plans with less than $200 million in assets are unavailable, so the extent to which these smaller plans invest in hedge funds and private equity is unclear.[21]

---

[21]In addition, Pyramis Global Advisors conducted a survey of plans with $200 million or more in total assets, but we found analysis of the *Pensions & Investments* and Greenwich Associates surveys sufficient for our purposes. See GAO-08-962 for analysis of the Pyramis Global Advisors survey data. According to Labor estimates, individual private DB plans with less than $200 million in total assets comprised about 15 percent of the total assets of all private DB plans in 2005. These small plans also comprised of about 97 percent of all DB plans in 2005.

Figure 3: Pension Plans with Investments in Hedge Funds and Private Equity by Size of Total Plan Assets in 2010

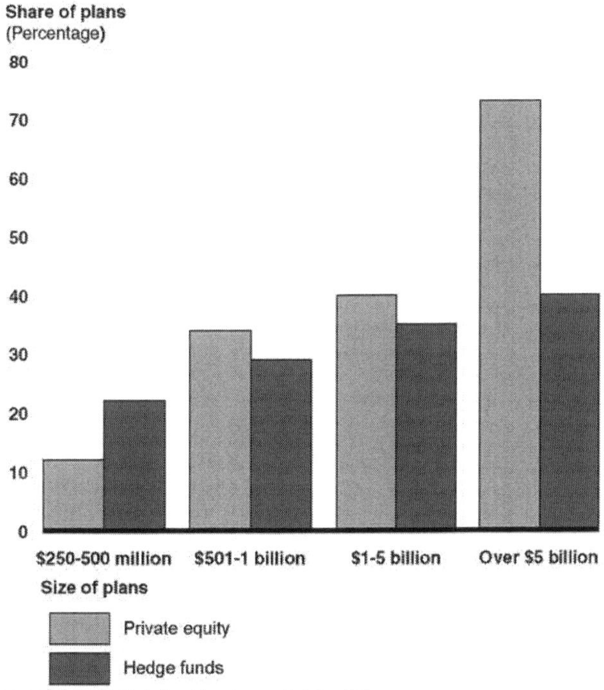

Source: Data provided by Greenwich Associates, 2010.

Note: The figure above includes public and corporate plans and does not include investments of collectively bargained plans.

Comments made to us by representatives of selected plan sponsors generally paralleled these national data. Of the 18 plans participating in our review that had invested in hedge funds, 17 told us they had either maintained or increased their allocations since our original contact in 2007 or 2008. For example, one public plan that already had invested a substantial percentage of its assets in hedge funds increased its investments by about another 10 percent of the total portfolio. Representatives of this plan explained that hedge fund investments, while not immune to stock market declines, had nonetheless performed much better than stocks during the financial crisis. Similarly, of the 22 plans participating in our review that had invested in private equity at the time of our original contact in 2007-2008, 19 told us that they had either maintained or increased their target allocation. Each of the 10 plans that had increased their allocations also cited positive performance returns. For example, one plan representative explained that the allocation to private equity had increased even though the overall allocation to publicly traded stocks has decreased. The representative explained that the plan was lowering its allocation to stocks as part of a broad risk reduction strategy, and that the additional return expected from private equity would therefore be essential. As the representative explained, this change was made with the belief that the increase in private equity will produce relatively high risk-adjusted returns and will therefore compensate for the lower expected yield resulting from the shift out of publicly traded stocks to bonds.

Most Plans Have Modified Investment Strategies in Recent Years

Experiences of recent years have led most plans we contacted to make significant changes to their hedge fund or private equity strategies, and in three cases, reductions in the overall allocation to hedge funds or private equity. For example, representatives of the one plan participating in our review that had reduced its overall allocations to hedge funds said that the plan's poor experience with hedge funds was tied to illiquidity. These representatives explained that they had expected that their hedge fund investments would not be difficult to cash in when they needed to pay obligations, but they were prevented from doing so by discretionary gates imposed by the fund manager. As a result, the plan was forced to sell stocks during the crisis when values were depressed, resulting in significant losses.

Changes to Hedge Fund Strategies

Several plans also discontinued or reduced the use of certain hedge fund strategies. For example, representatives of three plans told us that they had discontinued so-called "portable alpha" strategies, which commonly use hedge funds to help achieve returns that exceed those of the public equities market. According to industry press, this technique largely fell out of favor as a result of substantial investment losses during the 2008-2009 financial crisis. However, plan representatives indicated that disenchantment with the portable alpha technique did not necessarily mean abandonment of hedge funds generally. For example, after one of these three plans discontinued the portable alpha strategy, it opted to retain the hedge fund portion of the portable alpha investment.[22] Several other plans indicated that they invested in less aggressive hedge fund strategies. For example, a representative of one plan explained that the plan had shifted from hedge funds designed to deliver investment returns

---

[22]Portable alpha strategies can employ both hedge funds and other investment techniques in an effort to obtain returns above those of traditional benchmarks, such as the S&P 500.

that exceed the overall stock market to strategies that will deliver returns comparable to the stock market but with less risk.

In contrast to the general trend toward greater investments in hedge funds, some plans eliminated or substantially reduced their use of funds of hedge funds. Representatives of one plan explained that this step was part of a planned evolution—the plan had invested in funds of funds as a first step, and planned on using its relationships with funds of funds managers to develop the expertise to make direct hedge fund investments. By 2011, this plan had accomplished that objective, and 80 percent of its hedge fund investments were direct hedge fund investments. Another plan, however, discontinued funds of funds investments, concluding that funds of funds added an unnecessary layer of fees, offered the plan little opportunity to influence fees of underlying hedge funds, limited the plan's ability to conduct manager due diligence, and led to some overlapping investments in underlying individual hedge funds. A representative of this plan told us that one of the funds of funds had emphasized its unique access to top tier hedge funds, and the plan sponsor later learned that some of its other funds of funds were invested in the same vehicle, diminishing the diversification benefits of the fund of funds. However, funds of funds may be necessary for smaller pension plans and plans that lack well-developed internal investment and risk management that wish to invest in alternatives such as hedge funds and private equity.

Changes to Private Equity Strategies

Several plans indicated that they have adjusted their private equity strategies in recent years. For example, representatives of several plans noted that as a result of the experiences during the financial crisis, they preferred investing in private equity buyout funds that rely more on the implementation of operational improvements in portfolio companies, rather than funds that rely on so-called financial engineering—using leveraging techniques to enhance the value of the stock. One plan representative explained that many private equity firms using financial engineering techniques had suffered severe losses during the financial crisis. As a result, this representative said the plan now prefers private equity funds that add value to portfolio companies through means such as better control of costs, improved marketing, and a more efficient distribution chain. Also, because of the diminished returns of venture capital funds in recent years, representatives of several plans said they have reduced investments in such funds. Finally, several of the plans we contacted had made relatively short term, opportunistic investments in distressed debt as a result of the financial crisis. One plan representative explained that the financial crisis gave rise to this opportunity because distressed debt oriented funds tend to perform well in bad economic times as the universe of troubled companies grows and other investors become more risk-averse.

Some Plans Have Improved Contractual Terms or Changed Investment Arrangements

Steps plan sponsors have taken to obtain more advantageous terms when investing in hedge funds and private equity include lower fees, greater control and transparency, and changed liquidity terms.

More advantageous fee terms. A little more than half of the plans included in our review have taken steps to obtain more advantageous fee terms for both hedge fund and private equity investments. For example, as part of a broad policy change regarding its relationship with hedge fund managers, one large public plan has determined that it will seek to avoid investing in hedge funds that insist on the traditional "2 and 20" fee structure, under which investors pay an annual management fee of 2 percent of assets under management, and a performance fee of 20 percent of profits. Instead, the plan will seek to limit both management and performance fees and ensure that performance fees are paid not on an annual basis, but for more sustained, long-term performance. Representatives of another plan explained that they had obtained lower fees in exchange for trade-offs related to other aspects of investment terms. Specifically, for some hedge fund investments, this plan pays a flat fee of 1.5 percent of assets under management, instead of the formerly standard 2 percent fee. In exchange, the plan opted to sacrifice liquidity by agreeing to a 2-year lockup of its investment, thus providing the fund manager with greater assurance that its capital and investment strategies would not be disrupted. While illiquidity by itself may be perceived as a disadvantage to an investor, this plan believed less liquidity was a worthwhile trade-off for lower fees.

Principles developed by private equity investors. Large pension plans and other institutional investors in private equity have, through the Institutional Limited Partners Association (ILPA), taken significant steps to promote more advantageous terms of investment, including lower fees and better fee terms. The ILPA Private Equity Principles address in some detail how fees should be aligned to the interests of investors. For example, ILPA principles advocate a fee arrangement that would help ensure that investors get back all invested capital, plus a specified return on investment as soon as these returns are available. Sometimes referred to as a "European waterfall", this arrangement dictates that investors recover their full initial investment plus a specified return on investment—such as an annualized 8 percent—before the fund manager obtains any share of the profits.[23] This arrangement contrasts with an "American waterfall", under which the fund manager may collect profits corresponding to the sale of individual portfolio companies on a "deal by deal" basis, regardless of whether investors have obtained any return on their total investment in the fund. The overall advantage of the European waterfall for investors is that they can recapture their initial invested capital plus a specified return, as soon as that return exists, taking into account any losses. Further, because the fund manager does not obtain a share of the profits until after the investors have received the specified return, the need for reclamations of disbursements that have been made to the fund manager are minimized. Such reclamations—commonly referred to as "clawbacks"—may be necessary if profits paid to the fund manager based on the sale of portfolio companies early in the life of a fund are negated by subsequent losses. The ILPA Principles also address other issues, including notification of management changes and the fund management's financial stake in the fund.

Enhanced transparency, control, and liquidity through separate accounts. Many of the plans we contacted told us that some of the challenges of hedge fund investing could be addressed though the use of separate accounts in place of commingled funds. Under a commingled hedge fund arrangement, the investor owns a certain number of shares in the fund, but the hedge fund manager determines what assets to invest in, and the partnership collectively owns the underlying assets (see fig. 4). In contrast, under a separate account, the hedge fund manager essentially serves as a consultant who manages the assets in a way that generally parallels the hedge fund itself, but the investor may specify investment guidelines that result in differences between the commingled hedge fund and separate account. Plan representatives and financial industry experts cited multiple benefits of separate accounts, including (1) precise knowledge of the nature of underlying assets, (2) ability to exclude certain assets in the commingled hedge fund from its share of the rest of the hedge funds assets, and (3) much greater liquidity because plan sponsors own and can sell the underlying assets at will.[24] Separate

---

[23]A distribution "waterfall" is the method by which capital is distributed to funds investors as underlying investments are sold. The so-called "European" and "American" waterfalls are labeled as such because they reflect common practices in the respective markets.

[24]Plan officials explained that separate accounts can also be established for funds of hedge funds, or funds of private equity funds, in order to obtain benefits comparable to these described. For example, if a plan invests in a fund of hedge funds through a separate account, it can exclude an underlying hedge fund if it wishes.

account arrangements are, however, more costly than commingled funds, and hedge fund managers generally will not offer such arrangements unless the size of an investment exceeds a certain threshold.

Figure 4: Comparison of Commingled and Separate Accounts

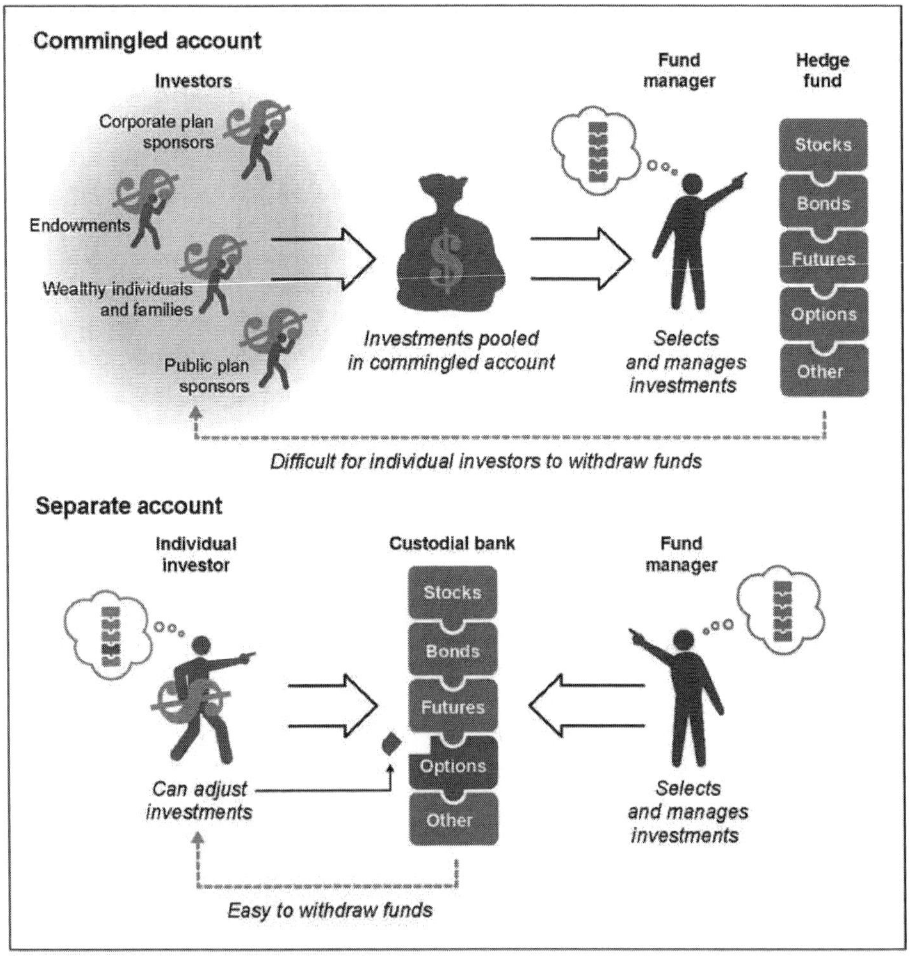

Source: GAO representation of industry descriptive information.

Note: Separate accounts may be established through a variety of arrangements. For example, in some cases the underlying assets will be held in the name of the investor and in other cases in the name of the fund manager in a dedicated account.

Other steps. Plan sponsor representatives also mentioned other steps they took to address difficulties of the last several years. Some plans now seek specific contractual terms that affect liquidity or other aspects of the investment. For example, representatives of one plan explained that they now seek investor level gates, under which cash-out limitations would be triggered once an investor has liquidated more than a specified amount of their investment. Other co-investors would not be affected and could still cash out under the normal terms of the hedge fund. Other plans have established certain criteria for selecting hedge fund or private equity funds. A representative of one plan, for example, said that the plan avoids hedge funds that have so-called side pockets—illiquid investments held separate from the primary fund—such as a hedge fund that has an investment in a private equity fund. A representative of one plan, which had been surprised by the existence of such side-pocket illiquid investments, noted that such investments can exacerbate illiquidity during stressful times. A representative of another plan noted that the plan prefers to select its own private equity investments and avoid locking in to one of a hedge fund manager's choosing. Finally, a few plans made changes to overall portfolio management practices as a result of experiences with hedge funds and private equity. For example, one plan established a larger cash reserve and representatives of two plans described steps to enhance or monitor liquidity.

Some Plans Described Investment Selection and Due Diligence Improvements, but Practices May be Uneven

A few plan representatives and experts described other improvements to their selection or monitoring processes for hedge funds or private equity investments. For example, two plan sponsors said they are much more focused on how fund managers establish the value of invested shares. One plan representative noted that, in the past, the plan took valuations provided by the fund manager at face value, but they now examine valuations much more closely. Representatives of other plans said that, as a result of massive hedge fund cash-outs by other co-investors, they consider the nature of other co-investors before investing. One plan representative explained that he prefers investors who will ride out market volatility and not flee the fund during episodes of volatility. Several surveyed experts cited diligence improvements, including better operational due diligence.[25]

---

[25]Operational due diligence involves examining operational risk, that is, the risk of investment loss due not to a faulty investment strategy, but from inadequate or failed internal processes, people and systems, or problems with external service providers. Such risk can arise from inexperienced operations personnel, inadequate internal controls, lack of compliance standards, or outright fraud.

Some public plans have also taken significant steps to improve and oversee the process of selecting hedge funds, private equity, and other investments. For example, a special review undertaken by one large public plan we contacted found significant problems involving the role of placement agents and accompanying malfeasance by public officials, which significantly compromised the plan's selection of private equity funds and other investment vehicles.[26] Among other things, the report raised the possibility that some private equity investments had been based on a relationship with a placement agent, rather than on the quality of the investment. Consequently, potentially superior investments may have been bypassed in favor of those with better connections, and the fund ultimately paid excessive fees that bore little or no relationship to the services rendered by the placement agent. The report's conclusions emphasized that plan officials must increase vigilance on those portions of the plan—such as hedge funds and private equity—that have not traditionally been subject to as great a degree of public scrutiny as other types of investments. The review also offered numerous recommendations designed to prevent a recurrence of these events, and the plan has taken some actions. For example, the plan has advocated, and the California state legislature has enacted, a state law that imposes on placement agents the same disclosure and registration requirements that apply to lobbyists, and obtained over $200 million in fee reductions and an agreement from elite money management firms to avoid using placement agents for new plan investments. Further, partly as a result of the review, the plan developed a comprehensive new policy designed to ensure that it had more advantageous terms of investment with its hedge fund managers. According to a representative of the National Association of State Retirement Administrators, other public plans have experienced similar problems and have made comparable reforms.[27]

---

[26] *Report of the CalPERS Special Review*, Steptoe and Johnson LLP and Navigant Consulting Inc., March 2011. Placement agents are intermediaries or middlemen paid by external money managers to help gain access to capital from institutional investors.

[27] The National Association of State Retirement Administrators is a nonprofit organization whose members are the directors of the nation's state, territorial, and largest statewide public retirement systems.

Plans May Have Limited Ability to Take Certain Steps

Although some plans have taken significant steps to improve the terms of hedge fund and private equity investments in recent years, not all plans may be able to take such steps, and it is not clear how extensive such changes have been. For example, separate accounts may not be a practicable option for all plan sponsors. Separate accounts impose additional duties on hedge fund managers and, therefore, the fees associated with them are often somewhat higher. In addition, they impose additional burdens on the investor, such as ensuring that the management of the separate account matches that of the commingled fund. Further, according to plan sponsors and experts, hedge fund managers will establish and operate separate accounts only for investments of a certain magnitude; hedge fund managers may not establish separate accounts for investments of less than approximately $100 million. As a result, separate accounts would not be an option for plans unable to make an investment of this magnitude.

Although our survey of experts identified some of the same actions that plan representatives described, the narrative responses revealed no clear pattern or consensus regarding these actions. Further, plan representatives and some experts indicated that not all plans would be able to take the steps described above. For example, plans' ability to obtain better fee terms is not universal. One plan representative noted that his plan is not large enough to have much negotiation power with fund managers, and the plan generally accepts the manager's standard fee structure. Another plan representative noted that the top fund managers have not had to adjust fees. Also, with regard to due diligence steps, some surveyed experts indicated that difficulties are likely to be among smaller plans or plans with lesser resources. For example, one respondent stated that while the use of best practices is becoming more widespread, failure to observe them occurs among smaller funds that lack resources or plans that are influenced by a salesperson.

Finally, it is not clear whether some of the changes in recent years will permanently change the landscape. One of the leading plan consultants noted that, since the financial crisis, plans have gained significant bargaining power with hedge fund managers who desire plan investments. However, representatives of two plans also indicated that this development may be cyclical, and an outgrowth of the troubled financial markets in recent years. These representatives also speculated that, when financial markets heat up again, the environment may change to a "seller's" market, and fund managers may be able to reassert fee structures and other investment terms that are less advantageous to investors.

Federal Entities and Others Have Developed Guidance Addressing Hedge Funds and Private Equity

Various entities have developed guidance applicable to plan investments in hedge fund and private equity, ranging from broadly applicable guidance issued by Labor to detailed guidance issued by federal advisory and industry bodies. While Labor has not developed guidance specifically addressing hedge funds or private equity, departmental officials cited a 1996 information letter from Labor to the Comptroller of the Currency that discusses the application of ERISA principles regarding the use of alternative investments.[28] The letter does not refer to hedge funds or private equity, but departmental officials said that its basic principles could be applied to these types of investments. The letter addresses pension plans' use of derivatives in their investment portfolios and states that investments in derivatives are subject to ERISA fiduciary responsibility rules, just as any other investment.[29] In light of this, the letter emphasizes several key considerations, including

- *Sophistication.* Such investments may require more sophistication and a deeper understanding on the part of fiduciaries than other investments.

- *Adequate information.* Fiduciaries are responsible for obtaining sufficient information to understand such investments and, if the investment is in a pooled fund managed by another entity, the fiduciary should obtain sufficient information to determine the nature of the pooled fund's uses of derivatives.

- *Understanding of investment risk.* The market risks of these investments should be understood and evaluated in terms of, among other considerations, the effect they have on the portfolio's overall risk.

- *Understanding operational and legal risk.* The fiduciary must determine whether it has adequate information and risk management systems in place given the nature, size, and complexity of the investment, and must ensure proper documentation of a derivative transaction.

---

[28]Letter from Department of Labor to the Comptroller of the Currency, March 21, 1996.

[29]Derivatives are financial instruments that are based on the price movements of underlying assets. Common types of derivatives include futures and options.

While Labor has issued this general guidance applying to investments in derivatives, other organizations have published guidance specifically encompassing or targeted at hedge fund and private equity. In December 2011, the Organisation for Economic Cooperation and Development (OECD) and the International Organisation of Pension Supervisors (IOPS) published a set of good practices for pension plans' use of alternative investments, including hedge funds and private equity.[30] Based on a survey of OECD and IOPS members, this document offers recommended good practices on issues such as investment policy, risk management, and contractual terms, as well as best practices for pension fund regulators. In 2009, the President's Working Group on Financial Markets[31] issued a report detailing important considerations and best practices for hedge fund investors, including specific guidance for fiduciaries.[32] This document provides basic background information about hedge funds, distinguishes them from more traditional investments, and outlines some of the basic considerations a fiduciary should make in the earliest stages of considering a hedge fund investment. The document also provides extensive guidance and suggestions for best practices related to due diligence steps, risk management, and various challenges involved in hedge fund investing, including valuation, fees and expenses, and legal and regulatory considerations, among other issues. Similarly, the Greenwich Roundtable, a nonprofit research and educational organization for investors in alternative assets, has issued a document that outlines due diligence best practices for alternative investments, including hedge fund and private equity investments.[33] This document

---

[30]OECD/IOPS, *Good Practices on Pension Funds' Use of Alternative Investments and Derivatives*, Organisation for Economic Cooperation and Development and International Organisation of Pension Supervisors (December 2011). IOPS is an international body representing those involved in supervision of private pension arrangements. Membership includes representatives from about 60 countries and territories. OECD consists of 34 member countries, and seeks to promote policies that will improve economic and social well-being.

[31]Established by executive order in 1988, the President's Working Group on Financial Markets is composed of top officials of the Department of the Treasury, the Board of Governors of the Federal Reserve, the SEC, and the Commodity Futures Trading Commission. (53 Fed. Reg. 9421, 3 C.F.R., 1988 Comp., p. 559).

[32]*Principles and Best Practices for Hedge Fund Investors: Report of the Investors' Committee to the President's Working Group on Financial Markets* (Jan. 15, 2009).

[33]*Best Practices in Alternative Investments: Due Diligence*, Education Committee of the Greenwich Roundtable (2010).

describes basic considerations in the process of considering any alternative investment, and it separately provides in-depth guidance on specific steps that should be taken in making hedge fund, private equity, and other illiquid investments.

In addition to these guidance documents, other organizations have published briefer guidance documents. In 2008, the Government Finance Officers Association published a brief advisory on the use of alternative assets by public employee retirement systems.[34] This three-page document presents a condensed explanation of the risks inherent in investing in hedge funds, private equity, and other alternative assets. It also highlights key due diligence considerations and recommends that state and local governments use extreme prudence in making such investments. More recently, the ILPA published a set of principles aimed at defined benefit pension plans and other institutional investors in private equity. This document details important aspects of the terms of investment between fund managers and investors, and best practices that fund managers and investors should observe during the course of the investment relationship.

In recent years, we and the ERISA Advisory Council have separately recommended that Labor take steps to help ensure that plans wishing to invest in hedge funds and private equity do so carefully.[35] In 2008, we recommended that the Secretary of Labor provide guidance to fiduciaries of ERISA Title I plans that would, among other things, outline the unique challenges of such investments, outline the steps plans should take to address these challenges, and highlight the implications of these challenges for smaller plans.[36] The ERISA Advisory Council has twice made comparable recommendations. In 2006, the council recommended that Labor publish guidance about the unique features of hedge funds

---

[34] *The Use of Alternative Investments for Public Employee Retirement Systems and Other Post Employment Benefit (OPEB) Established Trusts (2000 and 2008) (CORBA)*, Government Finance Officers Association (October 2008). The Government Finance Officers Association is a professional association of state, provincial, and local finance officers in the United States and Canada.

[35] The Advisory Council on Employee Welfare and Pension Benefit Plans, commonly referred to as the ERISA Advisory Council, was created by ERISA to provide advice to the Secretary of Labor. 29 U.S.C. § 1142.

[36] GAO-08-692.

and matters for consideration in their adoption for use by qualified plans.[37] While the council concluded that hedge funds may be an acceptable form of investment, its report noted that certain aspects of hedge fund investments should be brought to the forefront in educating plan fiduciaries and others. Among these are investment styles, liquidity issues, and potential conflicts of interest. In 2008, the council reviewed hard-to-value assets, which can include hedge funds, private equity, and other alternative assets.[38] [39] As a result of related hearings and deliberations, the council recommended that Labor issue guidance addressing the complex nature and distinct characteristics of such assets. The council further specified that the guidance should define hard-to-value assets and describe ERISA obligations when selecting, valuing, accounting for, monitoring, and reporting on these assets. To date, Labor has implemented neither our recommendations nor the council's recommendations. In responding to our 2008 recommendation, Labor noted that while it would consider the recommendation, the lack of uniformity among hedge funds and private equity funds could make development of comprehensive and useful guidance difficult.

In 2011, the ERISA Advisory Council specifically revisited the issue of pension plans' investments in hedge funds and private equity. The 2011 sessions of the council's hearings prominently considered the potential role of hedge fund and private equity investments in retirement plans. The council's report has not yet been published, but according to a Labor official, publication is expected in early 2012.

Concluding Observations

Plans and their hedge fund and private equity investments have not been immune to the effects of the financial market turbulence in recent years. Despite significant losses, however, DB plan sponsors and experts we contacted generally indicated that these alternative assets had met expectations and still had a significant role to play in the plans' investment

---

[37]U.S. Department of Labor ERISA Advisory Council, *Report of the Working Group on Prudent Investment Process* (November 2006).

[38]U.S. Department of Labor ERISA Advisory Council, *Report on Hard to Value Assets and Target Date Funds* (2008).

[39]Hard-to-value assets are those that are not listed on any national exchanges or over-the-counter markets, or for which quoted market prices are not available.

portfolios. Data from surveys of public and private plans clearly indicate that the appetite for such investments is continuing to grow.

Nonetheless, the events of the last 4 years have reinforced our 2008 observation that hedge funds and private equity also pose risks and challenges beyond those posed by more traditional investments. Representatives of some of the plans that we contacted indicated that hedge fund investments were less resilient than expected. As a result of poor performance or other issues related to hedge funds and private equity, some plans have taken significant steps to adjust the nature or terms of such investments. These steps will likely benefit the plans and, therefore, the plan participants and beneficiaries, in coming years.

Although some plans have taken significant actions, it is not clear how extensive such changes have been and whether such changes would be practical for those DB plans that lack both the resources and the negotiating power available to other plans. Our selection of 22 DB plans included some of the largest retirement plans in the nation, some of which manage tens of billions of dollars. Yet despite their size and expertise, some of these plans encountered significant difficulties with their alternative investments in recent years, resulting in substantial adjustments to plan investment practices. It is worth asking, if such large, sophisticated institutions can have difficulties that result in significant changes in the nature or terms of their investment in these alternative asset classes, how much more difficult it might be for medium and smaller plans.

In 2008, we recommended that the Secretary of Labor issue guidance designed for qualified plans under ERISA concerning alternative investment practices. We specifically called for guidance that would (1) outline the unique challenges of investing in hedge funds and private equity; (2) describe steps that plans should take to address these challenges and help meet ERISA requirements; and (3) explain the implications of these challenges and steps for smaller plans. We still believe that providing such guidance would be beneficial. In fact, in light of the guidance documents issued by other national and international organizations in the intervening years, this task might now prove easier for Labor than it would have been 4 years ago. Such guidance still has the potential to help plan sponsors, and our work suggests a continued need for such assistance.

Agency Comments

We provided a draft of this report to the Department of Labor, Department of the Treasury, the Pension Benefit Guaranty Corporation, and the Securities and Exchange Commission (SEC) for review and comment. Labor, the Department of the Treasury, and SEC provided technical comments which we incorporated as appropriate.

As agreed with your office, unless you publicly announce the contents of this report earlier, we plan no further distribution until 30 days from the report date. At that time, we will send copies of the report to the appropriate congressional committees, the Secretary of Labor, Secretary of the Treasury, the Director of the Pension Benefit Guaranty Corporation, Director of the SEC, and other interested parties. This report will also available at no charge on the GAO website at http://www.gao.gov.

If you or your staff have any questions regarding this report, please contact Charles Jeszeck at (202) 512-7215 or jeszeckc@gao.gov . Contact points for our Offices of Congressional Relations and Public Affairs may be found on the last page of this report. Key contributors are listed in appendix II.

Sincerely yours,

Charles Jeszeck, Director
Education, Workforce
 and Income Security Issues

Appendix I: Objectives, Scope, and Methodology

Our objectives were to answer the following research questions:

- What is known about the experiences of defined benefit pension plans with investments in hedge funds and private equity, including recent lessons learned?

- How have plan sponsors responded to lessons learned from recent experiences with such alternative investments?

- What steps have federal agencies and other entities taken to help plan sponsors make and manage investments in such alternative assets, and what additional steps might be warranted?

To answer all of the research questions, we conducted in-depth interviews with plan representatives of the private and public sector pension plans that were selected for our 2008 report examining the extent to which pension plans invest in hedge funds and private equity.[1] While 26 plans were interviewed for the 2008 report, 22 plans participated in follow-up interviews for our report (see table 3 for a list of plan officials we interviewed). We conducted interviews with representatives from June 2011 to September 2011 and, we obtained and reviewed available supporting documentation. These interviews were conducted using a semistructured interview format, which included open-ended questions on the following topics, asked separately about each plan's hedge funds or private equity investments: history of investment in hedge funds or private equity; experiences with these investments to date; lessons learned with these investments; changes made to address these lessons, including due diligence and ongoing monitoring; and actions federal agencies, such as Labor, should take to ensure that pension plan fiduciaries better make and manage their hedge fund and private equity investments. Four of the plans, who did not invest in hedge funds when we interviewed them for our 2008 report, were included in our in-depth interviews to determine whether plan representatives subsequently invested in hedge funds and to determine their experience given that decision. The results of the plan sponsor interviews were limited by plan representatives' willingness to speak with us.

---

[1]GAO-08-692.

Table 3: List of Pension Plans Interviewed

Interviewed for 2008 report	Interviewed for 2012 report
Private plans	
1. American Airlines	√
2. Boeing	
3. Exxon Mobil	√
4. GE Asset Management	√
5. International Association of Machinists National Pension Fund	√
6. John Deere	
7. Macy's	√
8. Northrop Grumman	√
9. Prudential	√
10. Target	√
11. United Mine Workers of America Health and Retirement Funds	√
12. United Technologies	√
13. Walt Disney	√
Public plans	
14. California Public Employees' Retirement System	√
15. California State Teachers' Retirement System	√
16. Illinois State Board of Investment	√
17. Los Angeles County Employee Retirement Administration	
18. Massachusetts Pension Reserves Investment Management Board	√
19. Missouri State Employees' Retirement System	√
20. National Railroad Retirement Investment Trust Fund	√
21. New York State Common Retirement Fund	
22. Pennsylvania Public School Employees' Retirement System	√
23. Pennsylvania State Employees' Retirement System	√
24. San Diego County Employees' Retirement Association	√
25. South Dakota Retirement System	√
26. Washington State Investment Board	√

Source: GAO.

Note: Four of the plans interviewed did not invest in hedge funds when we interviewed them in 2008.
One of these plans subsequently decided to invest in hedge funds.

The plans we interviewed were selected based on several criteria
identified in our 2008 report. Specifically, when these plans were selected
for our prior report, we attempted to select plans that varied in the size of
allocations to hedge funds and private equity as a share of total plan
assets. We also attempted to select plans with a range of total plan
assets, as outlined in table 4. We identified these plans using data from
the 2006 *Pensions & Investments* survey of the largest 200 pension plans
and through our interviews with industry experts. While we selected plans
representing a range of total plan assets and varying size of allocations to
hedge funds and private equity as a share of total plan assets, these plan
representatives' responses do not represent a statistically generalizeable
sample of all pension plans.

Table 4: Criteria Used in 2008 Selection of Plans for In-Depth Interviews

	Hedge funds	Private equity
Size of allocation to hedge funds or private equity		
None	5	
5% or less	10	5
>5 to 10%	3	6
>10%	2	2
Total plan assets		
$10 billion or less	8	5
>$10 to $100 billion	9	5
>$100 billion	3	3

Source: GAO analysis of *Pensions & Investments* 2006 survey.

To further address the research questions, we surveyed a selected group
of 20 experts in the areas of pension plan hedge fund and private equity
investment. We asked these experts five questions related to
performance and management of these funds during the past 5 years and
also requested suggestions, if any, for regulatory improvements.
Specifically, we asked how pension plans' hedge fund and private equity
investments have performed; lessons learned with respect to pension
plan hedge fund and private equity investments; changes to pension plan
hedge fund and private equity investment practices; the extent to which
pension plans observe best practices in hedge fund and private equity
due diligence; and actions federal agencies, such as Labor, should take
to ensure that pension plan fiduciaries better make and manage their

hedge fund and private equity investments. We used a Web-based form
to collect responses. This group of experts was selected from a number
of sources, including experts from our 2010 GAO Retirement Security
Advisory Panel, referrals from interviews and other experts, and
recommendations from GAO subject matter experts. To ensure we had a
range of views we invited participants from several different backgrounds
to participate in our survey including academics, representatives of public
and private plan sponsors, representatives of plan participants, pension
consultant groups, and other key national organizations and subject
matter experts. Of the 20 experts who agreed to participate in the survey,
19 completed the questionnaire within the requested time frame. The
survey was conducted in August 2011.

To quantitatively address national hedge fund and private equity
investment performance for the first question, we obtained and reviewed
broad industry performance data from two private organizations,
Cambridge Associates LLC and Hedge Fund Research, Inc.[2] Data from
these organizations captured historical hedge fund and private equity
investment performance, including performance at the peak of the
financial crisis. We used these data to determine broad hedge fund and
private equity performance over the last 5 years.

While the data from each of these organizations are limited in some ways,
we conducted data reliability assessments for each data source and
determined that the data were sufficiently reliable for purposes of this
study. Data from these organizations are not specific to pension plan
hedge fund and private equity investments, which may have different
investment performance due to specific investment terms and industry
access. Moreover, because these data were from broad investment
indexes, they neither illustrated differences in performance for various
investment strategies within hedge fund and private equity investments,
nor did they distinguish performance of fund of funds investment. While
the most informative way to assess how well investments have performed
is to analyze actual portfolio investment data, we were unable to
quantitatively analyze specifically how pension plans' investments in
hedge funds and private equity have performed over the past 5 years. We
attempted to obtain detailed investment performance data from selected

---

[2]Cambridge Associates LLC is a private and institutional investment consulting and
research firm and Hedge Fund Research, Inc. is an investment research firm specializing
in the areas of indexation and analysis of hedge funds.

custodian banks and investment consulting firms. These two groups have
data on the largest pension plan investments in the country. However,
because of the proprietary nature and considerable cost, both in
resources and expense, we were not able to conduct this analysis.

To address the second question, we obtained and analyzed survey data
of private and public sector defined benefit plans on the extent of plan
investments in hedge funds and private equity from two private
organizations, Greenwich Associates and *Pensions & Investments*.[3] We
identified these two surveys from prior work and obtained updated 2010
data.[4] As seen in table 5, the surveys varied in the number and size of
plans surveyed. Using available survey data, we determined the
percentage of plans surveyed that reported investments in hedge funds or
private equity. Using data from Greenwich Associates, we also
determined the percentage of surveyed plans that invested in hedge
funds or private equity by category of plan size, measured by total plan
assets. We further examined data from each survey on the size of
allocations to hedge funds or private equity as a share of total plan
assets. Using the Pensions & Investments data, we analyzed allocations
to these investments for individual plans and calculated the average
allocation for hedge funds and private equity, separately, among all plans
surveyed that reported these investments. The Greenwich Associates
data reported the size of allocations to hedge funds or private equity as
an average for all plans surveyed.

While the information collected by each of the surveys is limited in some
ways, we conducted a data reliability assessment of each survey and
determined that the data were sufficiently reliable for purposes of this
study. These surveys did not specifically define the terms hedge fund and
private equity; rather, respondents reported allocations based on their
own classifications. Data from both surveys are reflective only of the
plans surveyed and cannot be generalized to all plans.

---

[3]Greenwich Associates is an institutional financial services consulting and research firm
and *Pensions & Investments* is a money management industry publication.

[4]GAO-08-692.

Table 5: Number and Size of Pension Plans Observed in Recent Surveys

	Greenwich Associates (2010)	Pensions & Investments (2010)
Sample size	564 pension plans	131 pension plans
Total assets of plans in survey	$4.3 trillion[a]	$3.1 trillion
Range of total plan assets	$250 million or more	$1.7 billion or more

Sources: Greenwich Associates and *Pensions & Investments*.

Note: *Pensions & Investments* surveyed the largest 200 plans, ranked by combined defined benefit and defined contribution plan assets. Of the top 200 plans, 131 were defined benefit plans that completed the survey and provided asset allocation information. Greenwich Associates surveyed 590 plans; however, we excluded 24 unions and 2 endowments and foundations from our analysis.

[a]Total assets for the 564 surveyed private and public plans projected to approximately 1,200 private plans and 325 public plans.

To address the third question, we first reviewed relevant literature and spoke with federal officials from relevant agencies, including the Labor, the SEC, and the Pension Benefit Guaranty Corporation to understand federal agency action to date. In addition, we interviewed key national organizations and pension industry experts to understand the perspective of plan officials and their participants regarding federal actions to date, as well as then need for additional federal action. Key national organizations included representatives from organizations that represent plan participants, such as AARP, and an organization that represents plan officials, the American Benefits Council. In addition, we interviewed academic and national experts in the pension and alternative investment area and pension plan consultants. We also attended and participated in Labor's ERISA Advisory Council 2011 hearings on pension plan investments in private equity and hedge funds, including the use of these investments in defined contribution plans.[5] We reviewed and analyzed the detailed information collected through the literature review, discussions, and hearings to determine actions taken to date by federal agencies and other entities to help plan sponsors make and manage hedge fund and private equity investments.

We conducted this performance audit from February 2011 to February 2012 in accordance with generally accepted government auditing standards. Those standards require that we plan and perform the audit to

---

[5]GAO-11-901SP.

obtain sufficient, appropriate evidence to provide a reasonable basis for our findings and conclusions based on our audit objectives. We believe that the evidence obtained provides a reasonable basis for our findings and conclusions based on our audit objectives.

Appendix II: GAO Contact and Staff Acknowledgments

GAO Contact	Charles A. Jeszeck, Director, (202) 512-7215, or jeszeckc@gao.gov
Staff Acknowledgments	David Lehrer, Assistant Director, and Michael Hartnett, Analyst-in-Charge, managed this review. Amber Yancey-Carroll also led portions of the research and made significant contributions to all portions of this report. Kathleen van Gelder helped develop the structure of the report, and Luann Moy provided methodological assistance. Sheila McCoy and Roger Thomas provided legal assistance. Ashley McCall assisted in identifying relevant literature. James Bennett developed the report's graphics. Caitlin Croake and Lauren Gilbertson verified our findings.

GAO's Mission	The Government Accountability Office, the audit, evaluation, and investigative arm of Congress, exists to support Congress in meeting its constitutional responsibilities and to help improve the performance and accountability of the federal government for the American people. GAO examines the use of public funds; evaluates federal programs and policies; and provides analyses, recommendations, and other assistance to help Congress make informed oversight, policy, and funding decisions. GAO's commitment to good government is reflected in its core values of accountability, integrity, and reliability.
Obtaining Copies of GAO Reports and Testimony	The fastest and easiest way to obtain copies of GAO documents at no cost is through GAO's website (www.gao.gov). Each weekday afternoon, GAO posts on its website newly released reports, testimony, and correspondence. To have GAO e-mail you a list of newly posted products, go to www.gao.gov and select "E-mail Updates."
Order by Phone	The price of each GAO publication reflects GAO's actual cost of production and distribution and depends on the number of pages in the publication and whether the publication is printed in color or black and white. Pricing and ordering information is posted on GAO's website, http://www.gao.gov/ordering.htm. Place orders by calling (202) 512-6000, toll free (866) 801-7077, or TDD (202) 512-2537. Orders may be paid for using American Express, Discover Card, MasterCard, Visa, check, or money order. Call for additional information.
Connect with GAO	Connect with GAO on Facebook, Flickr, Twitter, and YouTube. Subscribe to our RSS Feeds or E-mail Updates. Listen to our Podcasts. Visit GAO on the web at www.gao.gov.
To Report Fraud, Waste, and Abuse in Federal Programs	Contact: Website: www.gao.gov/fraudnet/fraudnet.htm E-mail: fraudnet@gao.gov Automated answering system: (800) 424-5454 or (202) 512-7470
Congressional Relations	Katherine Siggerud, Managing Director, siggerudk@gao.gov, (202) 512-4400, U.S. Government Accountability Office, 441 G Street NW, Room 7125, Washington, DC 20548
Public Affairs	Chuck Young, Managing Director, youngc1@gao.gov, (202) 512-4800 U.S. Government Accountability Office, 441 G Street NW, Room 7149 Washington, DC 20548

Please Print on Recycled Paper.

Printed in Great Britain
by Amazon.co.uk, Ltd.,
Marston Gate.